thoughts of scob; I want to make you feel

Paul Easton

thoughts of scob; I want to make you feel ©
2024 Paul Easton

All rights reserved.

Presentation by *BookLeaf Publishing*

Web: www.bookleafpub.com

E-mail: info@bookleafpub.com

ISBN: 9789360944704

First edition 2024

Dedicated to my parents, Irene and Jim, the kindest and bravest humans I know.

My meteoric rock of a wee sister, Joanne.

My bambinos, Morgan and Cameron, whom I love more than anything I've ever known.

PREFACE

My name is Paul Easton and I want to introduce you to the thoughts of scob. Simply put, my desire is to make you feel through my writing. The beauty of poetry is that everyone can read the same verse, but it can mean something completely different to each individual person and how it relates to them and their experiences. I hope that these stories of my experiences can do just that for you.

I've written letters, journals, and secret scribbles throughout my life mixed with a thirst for meaningful quotes and song lyrics. It was only until after I experienced some painful life lessons in loss, hurt, anger, depression, and bipolar disorder that I realized that my purpose for writing was to heal my pain.

I write as therapy, to self-medicate, to hear my own voice… and most importantly to spill the overpowering abundance of rapid thoughts out of my mind and slowly bleed them onto the paper so I can take a breath, just for a moment until the next tornado of thoughts arrive. I write for me.

However… I'm not completely self-serving. I have learned that by sharing these thoughts it has helped many people in my life and even some I have never met. This for me is the ultimate. I am a giver and teacher by nature, I get that from my parents.

My writings speak to some directly, offering advice, a strong shoulder, inspiration, and sometimes just the comfort of knowing that they aren't suffering alone and that their feelings matter whatever they are. To paraphrase Alan Watts "There are no wrong feelings; only wrong reactions to the feelings felt"… so feel them!

When was the last time you let go and allowed yourself to listen to your unfiltered thoughts? To really feel them without self-judgement or guilt? Probably not in a long time… So take this adventure with me and truly let go, feel, let it bleed because that is when you are truly you!

Life is for living my friend. Do just that.

Enjoy the passage of time and the thoughts of scob.

my black dog

Have you met him?
Have you ever seen him?
Do you know of him?
He's big and strong and can run like the wind!
He sits by me, rarely leaving my side,
but sometimes when he's still he's hard to find.
He loves me, he's loyal to me, like so many
others that have not,
I can call him my best friend.
I feed him, sometimes too much and things that I
should not…
the kids fuss at that
To that I say "he has a short life, let him live it
with the good things and make it meaningful".
They stay unamused.

I take him with me many places, many places I
should not,
He protects me, he is the one that won't leave
me.
My black dog.

Most mornings he wakes me as I struggle to get
out of bed,
He's so heavy as he sits on top of me, I just can't
get up.
I'm going to be late I tell him,
He cares not.
I don't feel like moving, I don't really care about
much.
I pet him to ease the pain,
But I lay here still hating everything and every
fucking one.
I know he has my back and he is loyal to me,
I love him and he loves me.
If someone was to come for me,
If I was to feel attacked,
If someone hurts me,
He will attack!
He will rip them to shreds,
He will rip them.. the fuck apart.
My black dog.

As I hurt yet another heart,
With vicious words, defense, and attack.

My black dog is there for me when others are
not
Fuck, he has ripped so much apart…
She looks at me behind teared eyes
"Can I meet him?" She asks
"Who" I said, feeling confused
"Your black dog" she said,
I looked at her with despair… "My dear… you
already have".

For all of us who have a black dog within us…

For the dark days and the darker nights please
know that things will change, it will pass, please
know it will pass. Take things one step at a time,
if that means all you can manage somedays is to
get up and brush your teeth, then do it, and the
next day do a little bit more, but you must know
that there are people who can and want to help.

These are written on my bathroom mirror so I
see them every morning I brush my teeth: "Pain
is inevitable. Suffering is optional" and "The
devil can scrap but the lord has won"

I have lost so much and so many because I have
constantly given into fear and hurt and let my
black dog take over with his primal protective
instinct and push those I care for far far away.

Understand that he is protecting you but you
have to learn and teach that part of yourself how
to accept pain and how to respond to hurt. This
is a process but one you must learn.

Love,

- scob

falling tears

Tears will fall,
But not from my dry eye,
I won't see them coming,
For I will look away.

Tears will fall,
But that doesn't mean I will for you this time,
I have to be cold,
Even when you are warm.

Are they still falling?
I hope they are,
Not because I hate you,
But so I can wipe them from your eye.

– scob

I feel fucking nothing

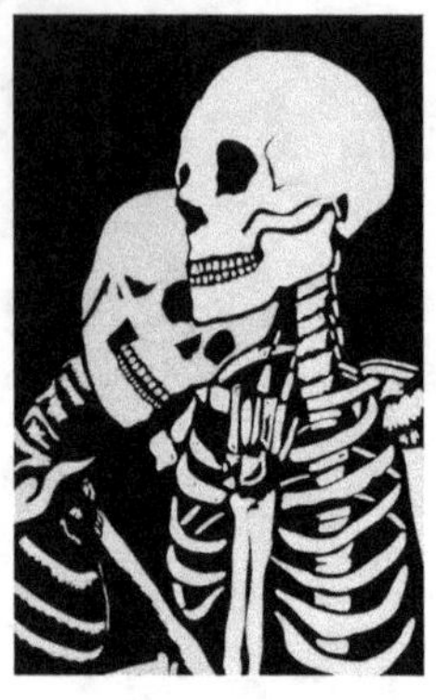

I feel nothing,
Absolutely nothing.
That's a lie,
I do feel,
I feel numbness, I feel it all the time.
Numbness to everything,
To the eye, to the touch, to my soul.

I feel the moments around me,
Ones I have ached for,
Pass through my hands like sand,
Like I was never there.
I can only watch the moment in my mental
replay,
As I anger that I never got to experience it,
I don't know what the moment felt like,

Only the memory of what it may have.

I feel the emptiness of my gaze as I look at those
I love and need,
I feel their confusion, fear, and hurt as they look
back at me.

You ungrateful cunt,
I'm not ungrateful I swear!
I care deeply but I just can't feel what I want to
feel,
I can't be where I need to be.

Please help me,
I don't want life to pass me by,
I don't care how long I have,
Even if it's moments,
I just want to feel.

– scob

the genius disease

She said I wasn't well,
But I felt fine.
I just need to get this part out,
These words swirling in my mind.
Why wasn't she listening,
I need her to hear,
To understand.

My tongue ready at the trigger,
Please just let me say these last few words,
I need them off my chest,
No, these are different words this time.

I need you to hear me,
I don't want your reaction,
Yes it matters but I can't consume,

Please you aren't hearing me,
Please you don't understand.

I'm up at night again,
My focus isn't there,
It isn't anywhere,
But on this one thing.
I'm all in,
But only on the words I need to say.
The road ahead I cannot see,
I can only stay right here at this part.
I don't want to stay here,
As I know there's so much good around us,
But I have to,
They don't matter right now,
Only my thoughts matters so fucking much.
You don't understand,
Please, we must stay,
Are you still there?

– scob

to my fellow insomniacs

In the wee hours of the morning,
When the silence is loudest,
When your thoughts are heaviest,
You mustn't shy away from them,
These are the hours that you must face.

Thoughts…
Finally free from distraction,
Let them flow,
Let them stay a while,
Listen without judgement,
Your judgement, that's what counts.
Soon you will know.

Be brave,
Now you will know.

– scob

if they cared enough

If they cared,
They would reach out.
You can think about all that you didn't do,
The dumb stuff you said,
Trust me if they cared enough they would.

How many more passive-aggressive moves can
you make,
Hoping and looking for subliminal messages,
How much more will you lie to yourself,
Trust me if they cared enough they would.

Yes, I'm sure they are going through things,
Who isn't?
I'm not saying they didn't ever care,
They once were all in,

I'm saying they don't care right now.

Stop hanging around,
Waiting, and hoping,
For them to want to see you,
To call, to text, to send funny memes again,
For them to fucking care about you.

It doesn't have to be forever,
But it certainly needs to be for right now.
You have to be about you now,
It's not selfish,
It's what's needed,
Trust me if you cared enough YOU would.

– scob

the ocean

We jumped in the waves,
So big and so strong,
Waiting on them to peak,
We stood hand in hand,
To meet them at their crest.

Some would lift us up high,
Others we couldn't beat,
So we had to let go for a moment,
I would duck and hold my breath,
As I watched you dive right through.

The ocean roared,
How can something so loud be so peaceful?
Even gave me hope.
You smiled at me and I smiled back,
But I wasn't really there.

The ocean is the greatest teacher of how to let go,
To swim with the tide and never against,
The same wave never lasting.

I just couldn't let go,
And now I can't find you,
I'm still lost at sea.

- scob

let it bleed

I know why you aren't performing,
You think you do but you don't.
Scared of the thoughts of others?
No that's not it.
Scared of failing?
Still not it.

It is because you are holding back,
You don't know that you are,
Subconsciously you shackle your skills,
And tidy away your talent.

You write, you play, you perform,
Only for them and never for you,
To make sure they like it,
Seeking validation,
Scared to offend,
Craving approval.

That way can't be your best,
It just can't.

Fuck, you know it's not!
Stop holding back,
That's not what you really want to put out,
It's just to please them.
That's not what your passions burn white hot
for,
Let go of what you think they want,
Without apology show them who the fuck you
really are.

It won't be easy at first, but that's the real
performance,
The performance of letting go.

Play your way,
Let it flow,
Let it bleed,
Until it's all that you can feel.

- scob

I don't miss you,
Certainly not all the time.
I don't wonder what you're doing,
Or care that you are no longer mine

Move on...
No, I miss your smile,
Let you go,
No, I miss making you laugh,
Plenty more fish in the sea,
I miss how you say my name.

I crave you all the time,
You are what keeps me up at night,
What zones me out during the day,
I crave you like you were still mine.

Your care,
The way you laugh,

Your scent,
Your warm heavy touch.

It's all I think about,
Even when I'm pretending you don't exist,
A million places I go,
None feel like you.

Only you and I existed in the crowded room,
Sneaking smiles,
Gentle touches when no one was looking,
Why can't it just be me and you.

The pain of losing you,
Is nothing compared to the pain of needing you.

- scob

feel

petrified of my own standards,
go right ahead,
read who is my mind.

I feel everything.
Every move, every step, every lyric, every word.
What do you feel?
I feel the same, but I don't feel the same.

-scob

8

Let your thoughts bleed out,
Bleed them onto this paper,
Let them soil your chest,
Soak everything with your tears.

Leave the wound open this time,
Let it pour,
Stop holding them in,
You are worth so much more.

- scob

you don't at all

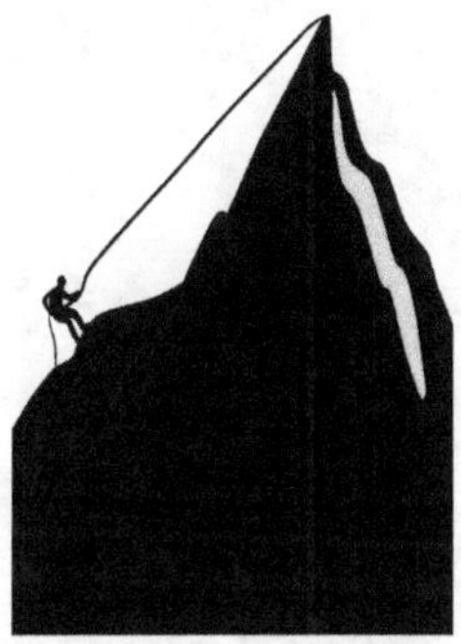

You think you need someone to tell you what to
do.
You think you need that quote, that sign.
You don't. You don't at all.

You already know what you want.
You are just finding ways to think your way out
of it.
Because it's scary.
Fucking right it's scary.

Slow it down.
Hear yourself think.
Trust yourself for once.
Now go live.
That's what life is for.

- scob

beach views

I went to the beach today,
All my worries in tow,
Feeling the sand on my feet,
I stood there hoping to feel something more.

My woes felt so heavy,
Worried I might sink,
Wishing I could empty my mind,
As the cool breeze brushed my face.

The crashing of the waves behind me,
Head down swimming in my thoughts,
I walked towards the ramp that took me to my
car.

There a man's face so calm met me with a smile
and a gentle nod,
His eyes fixed on mine like he saw right through
me,
I lifted my head to nod back, struggling to break
a smile.

Guilt slapped me hard in the face,
A sense of shame seeped in,
Thoughts started to clear as I walked away,
I now knew why I was there.
I turned for one last look at the coastline,
Hoping this time for a different view.
There on the ramp the man still sat,
Turning the hand rims on his wheelchair to face
the woman he was with,
He pointed to the sea as he gently touched her
hand,
They laughed together.

I drove home now smiling,
No thoughts but one,
Silence on the radio,
Perspective had now come.

- scob

you are not immune

I am just sad.
Everything has lost its taste,
I feel nothing,
Nothing for anyone or anything.
I am no longer present,
Not for me, not for anyone.
I am the thief of my own joy,
Nothing matters.

I cancel plans,
I don't show up,
I am faded out,
My friends don't understand,
I fear I will lose them soon.
Many leave me,

Those that I have loved.
Can I blame them?
No, but I will.

All I hear is silence,
The silence that deafens me,
Thoughts won't let me away, not even for a
moment to enjoy for someone else,
They want to keep me nestled in the thorns,
I want out.
I want to be free, but it's so fucking hard and
painful to pull away
I will stay here,
I will just stay here.

Everything just fucking hurts,
I feel nothing but yet I feel every pain,
Every nudge, every word, every comment.
I can't get happy, I can't feel happy, I feel
fucking numb,
Nothing matters, nothing counts, nothing feels
the same.
I just want to hear myself think again.
Me… not the voices weighing me down.

My head feels so heavy on this pillow, get up,
Please just get up, for you, for them, please,
They don't understand, none of them, how could
they…

I am scared, I am hurt, I am angry, I am lonely,
I need you, I need me again.

Fuck, it's all so heavy,
I want to get up,
Time slows down and for once I don't want it to.
How do I get up…

- scob

who are you sleeping with?

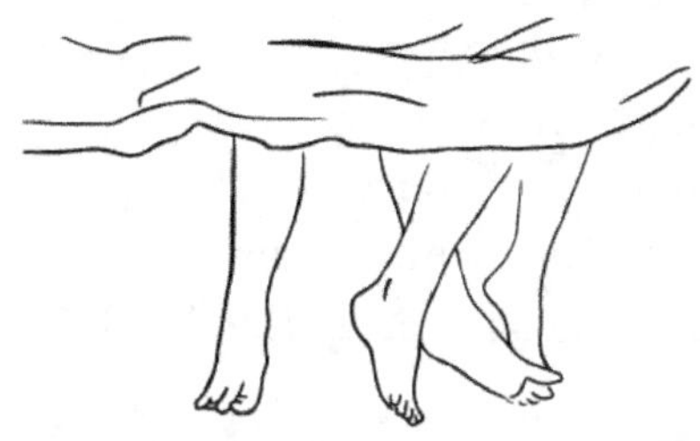

Who are you sleeping with?
Who have you let in your bed?
Why them? Them in particular?
How much space are they taking?

Do you even like them?
You seem irritated,
Pissed off,
Regretful.
Do you feel guilt?
Are you being honest with them?
Should they not be there?
Are you being honest with yourself?

Who else is sleeping in that bed?
Do they know?

Why do you turn over to look at your phone
when they fall asleep?
Why do you look towards the door?
Are you with the one whose attention you seek?

You aren't sleeping well,
It's starting to show.
It's you that keeps you awake,
It's you that can't settle to slumber,
It's you that is confused and can't rid of your
rage,
It's you that sleeps with you,
It's you that sleeps in your bed.

Who are you sleeping with?
The answer is and always will be… you.

Pour into you,
Understand what is bad,
And what is good,
Accept what has become,
And know what you must change.
You are what matters,
Make sure your best rest is with you.

– scob

the beautiful game

It wasn't the strike,
It wasn't the graceful turn,
Not the speed,
Nor the power,
It was the perfect touch of the outside of the foot
that guided the ball.

Caressed it,
Kissed it,
Made love to it,
Heavy light, light heavy,
The sound of leather on leather.
Control absolute.

Head up,
Starts to see in slow motion,
Can I squeeze it through?

Is he seeing what I'm seeing?
Thinking what I'm thinking?
Where the defender is,
Where the defender isn't.

Freshly cut,
You breathed air back into me,
Take the shot.
Jogo Bonito

The beautiful game

-scob

just you

You feel you are sinking,
Grasping for the ledge,
About to go under,
Is this your last breath.

Be still,
Don't panic,
Stop trying to save yourself,
This is when to be calm.

You have you,
All along you had you.

- scob

perspective

I travelled to gain perspective,
Overwhelmed and lost.

I cleared my mind,
Made room to roam,
Shed the doubt.

Stripped away the coats of who I have needed to
be,
Slowly removed the mask,
It was me you see.

Now I realize,
I had travelled to lose perspective.

- scob

kama

I'm not special,
Nothing unique.
I'm not special,
How could I be?
I'm just plain, plainly bare,
While fruitful others are everywhere.

Why the hell would I be?
How could I ever steal your pretty eyes?
What can I offer that you haven't already seen?
While others quench your thirst in ways that I
cannot.

Maybe the depths of me,
What's in my soul,
The way I think and love,
Care and give,
Can be enough for you,
Or is the shallow surface of others too strong to
ignore.

Your eyes devour what your temptation desires,
Turn away,
Glance back at me,
I'm so much deeper than them.

Will I ever be enough?
Or will you see temptation through?
Don't.
Make me special to you.

- scob

the dancer

As the dancer takes the stage to perform,
She feels the heat of the lights,
The silence of the crowd,
She sees no faces.

Does she need them to understand…?
The hours and hours of rehearsal,
The impeccable timing,
The scars and bruises on her feet,
The sacrifice,
The time and money spent,
The dedication,
The shattered dreams,

No…

She only needs them to feel.

Forgetting the faceless,
Letting go of all thought,
Dancing her every move,
Her soul on fire.

- scob

green eyes

My insecurity soars to the heavens,
Your words can't stop it in flight.
It's them not you,
Who makes me doubt.

You don't believe me,
I know.
For there's a monster inside me,
One I never want to let out.

Jealous anger rising,
Calm far gone,
Rushing to my defense,
The monster stepped in.

He punched the wall,

Feeling nothing but numb,
He only saw his pain,
Never your tears.

Hurt starts to fade,
I feel scared,
the monster gone,
I was all alone.
-    scob

can we?

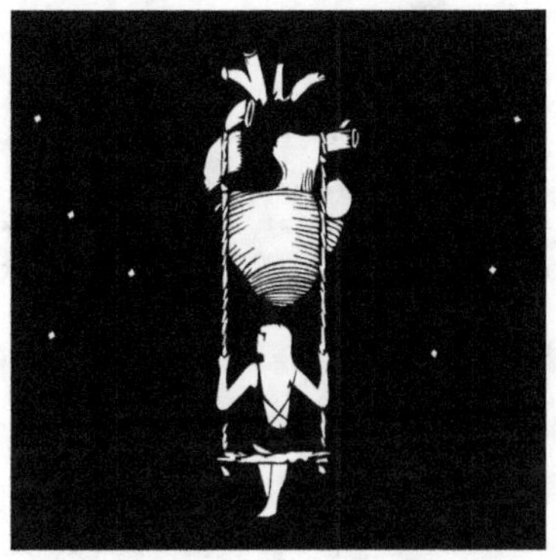

Why can't we make this work?
Just love each other,
Why can't we put it all aside?
The things that just don't matter.

Both of us clinging so tightly to fear,
While craving each other's touch,
Fighting to be near,
Loving you so much.

Okay, I'm going to tell you how I feel,
Say what I desperately need.
We meet with our eyes,
Panic floods my thoughts.

I can't…

I grab back on to fear.

-    scob

anger

So angry,
Filled with rage,
The water choppy,
Nothing could be seen.

With anger I screamed,
The water grew rougher,
Losing all sight,
Just nothing.

Exhausted I fell to the ground,
Drained completely,
I looked one last time,
To find the water was still,
Clear as the day,
I now see all that was written.

Be still.

- scob

do you mind

Don't try and stop them,
The thoughts that rush in,
In fact, hold the door wide open,
Welcome all…
As weird and wonderful as they are.

Sit back as they bounce around,
Hear them play,
Now open the backdoor of your mind,
Letting them leave,
Don't try to catch them,
Don't hold on.

The space that is left,
The clear you feel,
That's yours to fill,
Or not…

- scob

www.ingramcontent.com/pod-product-compliance
Lightning Source LLC
LaVergne TN
LVHW050948200726
843508LV00011B/2478